HAL•LEONARD®

BASS

PLAY-ALONG

MODERN WORSHIP

VOL. 37

CONTENTS

T0131122

To access audio visit:
www.halleonard.com/mylibrary

1537-6515-2892-1956

ISBN 978-1-61780-432-8

Visit Hal Leonard Online at
www.halleonard.com

Contact us:
Hal Leonard
7777 West Bluemound Road
Milwaukee, WI 53213
Email: info@halleonard.com

In Europe, contact:
Hal Leonard Europe Limited
42 Wigmore Street
Marylebone, London, W1U 2RN
Email: info@halleonardeurope.com

In Australia, contact:
Hal Leonard Australia Pty. Ltd.
4 Lentara Court
Cheltenham, Victoria, 3192 Australia
Email: info@halleonard.com.au

Above All

Words and Music by Paul Baloche and Lenny LeBlanc

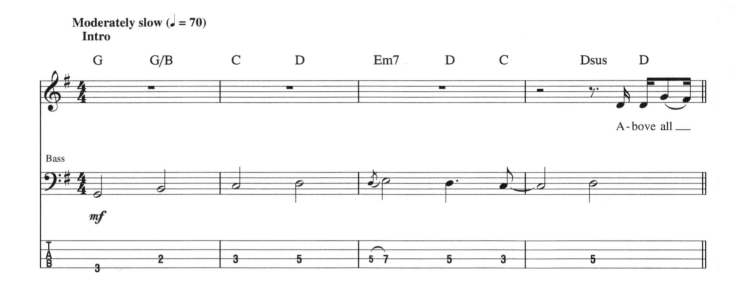

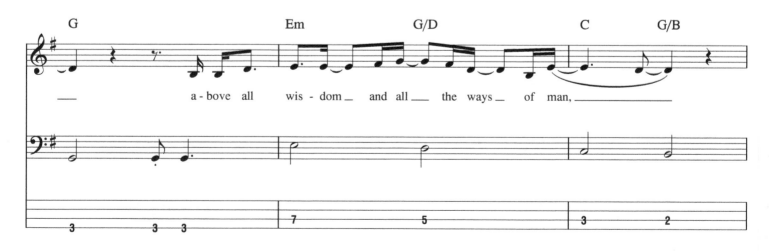

Days of Elijah

Words and Music by Robin Mark

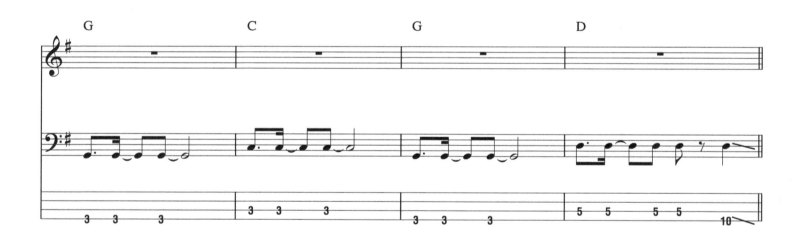

Holy Is the Lord

Words and Music by Chris Tomlin and Louie Giglio

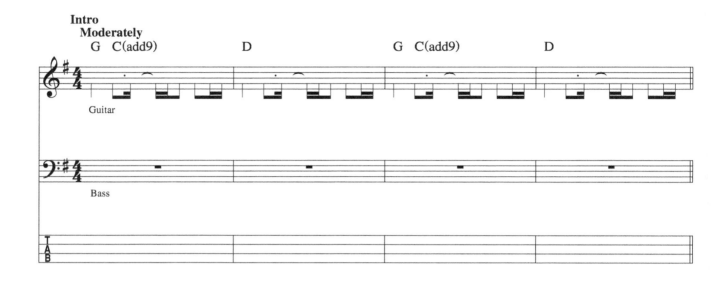

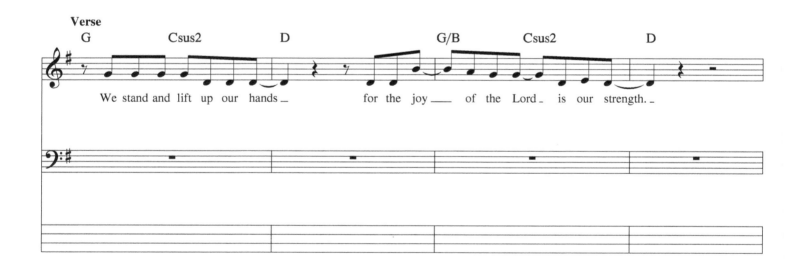

We stand and lift up our hands ___ for the joy ___ of the Lord ___ is our strength. ___

We bow down ___ and wor - ship Him now. ___ How great, ___ how awe - some is He. ___

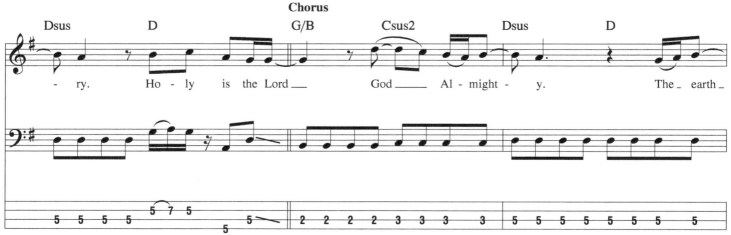

I Give You My Heart

Words and Music by Reuben Morgan

In Christ Alone

Words and Music by Keith Getty and Stuart Townend

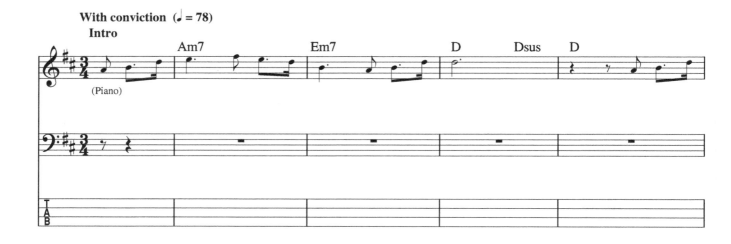

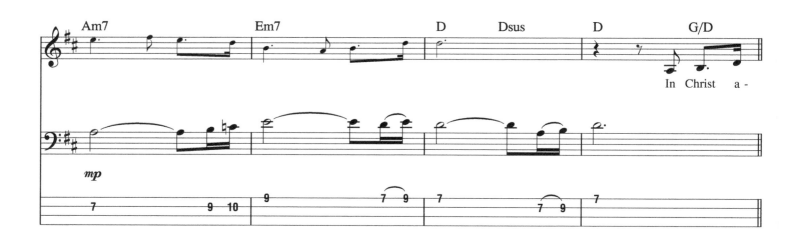

Let Everything That Has Breath

Words and Music by Matt Redman

praise —— You when I'm young and when I'm old.

Praise —— You when I'm laugh - ing, —— praise —— You when I'm griev - ing, ——

praise —— You ev - 'ry sea - son of the soul. —— If

C Pre-Chorus 1

we could see how much You're worth, Your pow'r, Your might, Your

Open the Eyes of My Heart

Words and Music by Paul Baloche

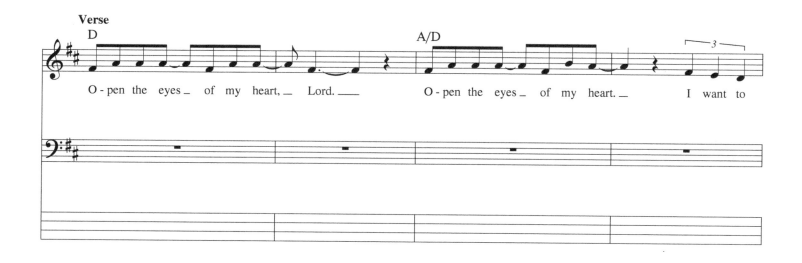

Worthy Is the Lamb

Words and Music by Darlene Zschech

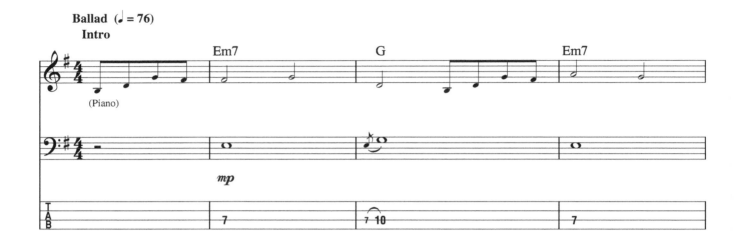

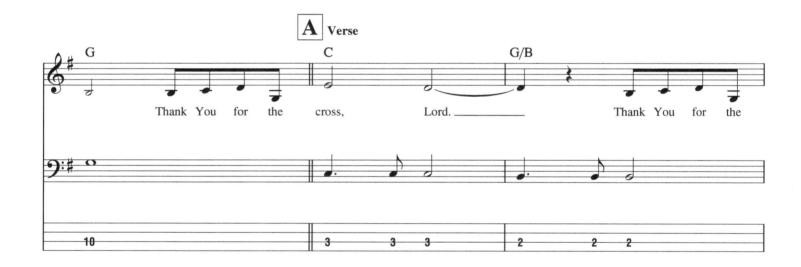

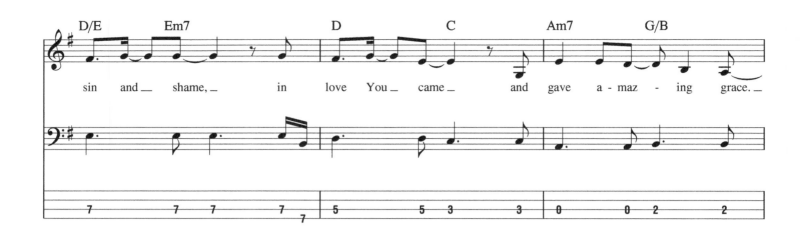

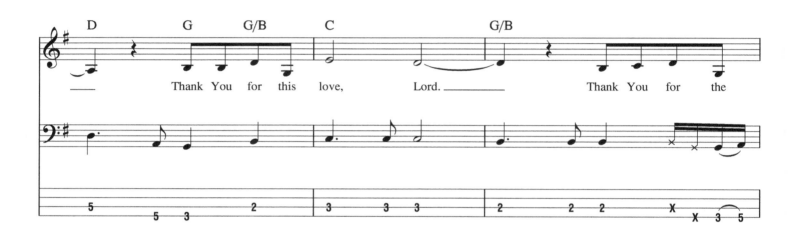

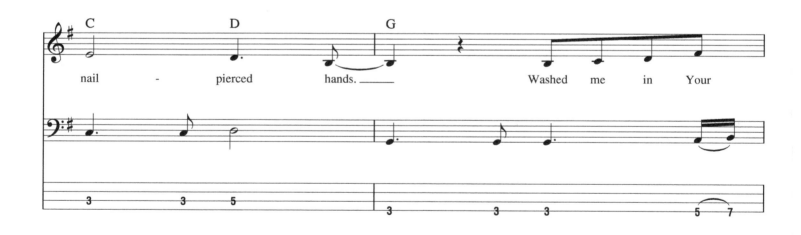

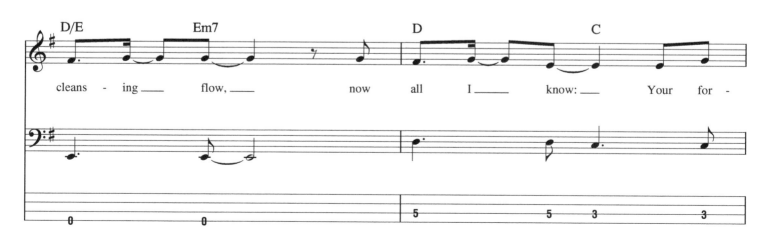

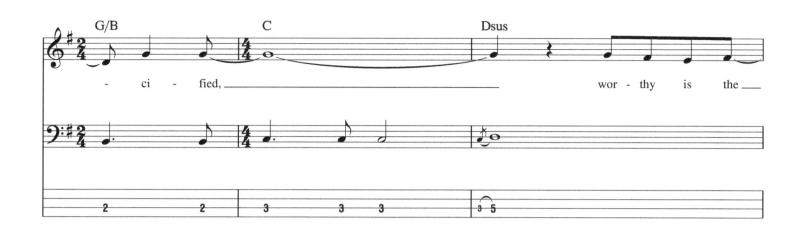

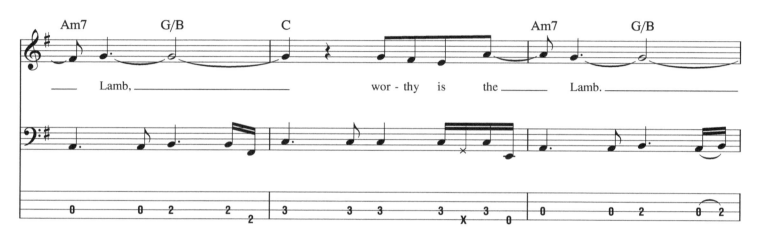

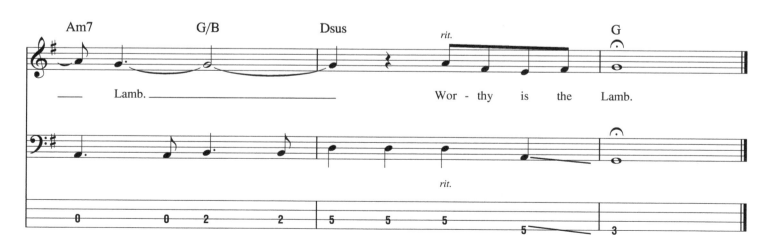

ABOVE ALL

PAUL BALOCHE and LENNY LeBLANC

Key of **G Major**, 4/4

INTRO:

G   G/B   C   D   Em7   D   C   Dsus   D

VERSE:

```
        C      Dsus          G
Above all powers,     above all kings
        C         Dsus        G
Above all nature and all created things
        Em        G/D            C    G/B
Above all wisdom and all the ways of man
Am7                          Dsus    D
You were here before the world began
        C        Dsus          G
Above all kingdoms,     above all thrones
        C          Dsus        G
Above all wonders the world has ever known
        Em        G/D            C    G/B
Above all wealth and treasures of the earth
Am7                              B7
There's no way to measure what You're worth
```

CHORUS:

```
G    Am7   D            G
Crucified,   laid behind a stone
    G     Am7    D          G
You lived to die    rejected and alone
      Em   G/D           C    G/B
Like a rose trampled on the ground
          Am7  G/B                C    Dsus
You took the fall        and thought of me
        G   G/B  C   Dsus  D
Above all  (C/E  D/F#)
```

(REPEAT VERSE)

(REPEAT CHORUS 2X)

TAG:

```
D/F#  Em  G/D              C    G/B
Like a rose trampled on the ground
          Am7  G/B                C    Dsus
You took the fall        and thought of me
        G   G/B  C   Dsus  D   G (hold)
Above all
```

DAYS OF ELIJAH

ROBIN MARK

Key of **G Major, 4/4**

INTRO (2X):

G C G D

VERSE 1:

G   C   G   D   G
These are the days of Elijah, declaring the word of the Lord

   G   C   G   D   G
And these are the days of Your servant Moses, righteousness being restored

   Bm   Em   Am   C   Dsus D
And though these are days of great trials, of famine and darkness and sword

  G   C   G   D   G
Still we are the voice in the desert crying, "Prepare ye the way of the Lord!"

CHORUS:

  D   G   C
Behold, He comes, riding on the clouds

               G   D
Shining like the sun at the trumpet call

         G   C
Lift your voice, it's the year of Jubilee

               G   D   G   (C G D)
And out of Zion's hill salvation comes

VERSE 2:

   G   C   G   D   G
And these are the days of Ezekiel, the dry bones becoming as flesh

   G   C   G   D   G
And these are the days of Your servant David, rebuilding a temple of praise

  Bm   Em   Am   C   Dsus D
And these are the days of the harvest, the fields are as white in Your world

  G   C   G   D   G
And we are the laborers in Your vineyard, declaring the word of the Lord

(REPEAT CHORUS 3X)

TAG:

D   G   C
Lift your voice, it's the year of Jubilee

             G   D   G (hold)
And out of Zion's hill salvation comes

HOLY IS THE LORD

CHRIS TOMLIN and LOUIE GIGLIO

Key of **G Major**, 4/4

INTRO (GUITAR ONLY):

G Csus2 D

G Csus2 D

VERSE:

G   Csus2   D
We stand and lift up our hands

    G/B   Csus2   D
For the joy of the Lord is our strength

G   Csus2   D
We bow down and worship Him now

G/B   Csus2   D
How great, how awesome is He

       A7sus   Csus2
Together we sing

CHORUS:

      G/B Csus2 Dsus D
Holy is the Lord God Almighty

   Em7   Csus2   Dsus
The earth is filled with His glory

D   G/B Csus2 Dsus D
Holy is the Lord God Almighty

   Em7   Csus2   Dsus D
The earth is filled with His glory

   Em7   Csus2   Dsus D
The earth is filled with His glory

(REPEAT VERSE & CHORUS)

BRIDGE:

   G   D/F♯
It's rising up all around

       F   C
It's the anthem of the Lord's renown

   G   D/F♯
It's rising up all around

       F   C
It's the anthem of the Lord's renown

            A7sus   Cadd2
And together we sing

       A7sus   Cadd2
Everyone sing

(REPEAT CHORUS)

(REPEAT LAST LINE OF CHORUS)

END ON G

I GIVE YOU MY HEART

REUBEN MORGAN

Key of **D Major, 4/4**

INTRO:

Gmaj7   A/G   F#m7   Bm7
Gmaj7   A/G   F#m7   G/A

VERSE:

D   A/C# Bm7
This is my de - sire

    G   D   A
To hon - or You

Bm7   A/C#   D
Lord, with all   my   heart

          Cmaj7   G   A
I worship You

D   A/C#   Bm7
All I have with - in me

  G   D   A
I give You praise

Bm7   A/C#   D
All that I a - dore

    Cmaj7   G   A
Is in You

CHORUS:

D   A
Lord, I give You my heart

             Em7
I give You my soul

 G/A
I live for You alone

D   A/C#
Ev'ry breath that I take

               Em7
Ev'ry moment I'm awake

    G/A   (Gmaj7   A/G   G/A)
Lord, have Your way in me

(REPEAT VERSE)

(REPEAT CHORUS 2X)

OUTRO:

Gmaj7   A/G   F#m7   Bm7
Gmaj7   A/G   F#m7   G/A   D (hold)

IN CHRIST ALONE

KEITH GETTY and STUART TOWNEND

Key of **D Major**, 3/4

INTRO (2X):

Am7   Em7   D Dsus D

VERSE 1:

  G/D   D   G   A
In Christ alone my hope is found

D/F♯   G   Em7 Asus   D
He is my light, my strength,   my song

  G/D   D   G   A
This Cornerstone, this solid ground

D/F♯   G   Em7 Asus   D
Firm through the fiercest drought and storm

   D/F♯   G   D/F♯   A
What heights of love, what depths of peace

   D/F♯   G   Bm7   A
When fears are stilled when strivings cease

  G   D   G   A
My Comforter, my All in All

D/F♯   G   Em7 Asus   D
Here in the love of Christ   I stand

(Dsus D)

VERSE 2:

In Christ alone, who took on flesh
Fullness of God in helpless Babe
This gift of love and righteousness
Scorned by the ones He came to save
'Til on that cross as Jesus died
The wrath of God was satisfied
For ev'ry sin on Him was laid
Here in the death of Christ I live

INTERLUDE:

Am7   Em7   D Dsus D

VERSE 3:

There in the ground His body lay
Light of the world by darkness slain
Then bursting forth in glorious day
Up from the grave He rose again!
And as He stands in victory
Sin's curse has lost its grip on me
For I am His and He is mine
Bought with the precious blood of Christ

(Dsus D)

VERSE 4:

No guilt in life, no fear in death
This is the pow'r of Christ in me
From life's first cry to final breath
Jesus commands my destiny
No pow'r of hell, no scheme of man
Can ever pluck me from His hand
'Til He returns or calls me home
Here in the pow'r of Christ I'll stand

TAG:

  D/F♯   G   D/F♯   A
No pow'r of hell, no scheme of man

  D/F♯ G   Bm7   A
Can ever pluck me from His hand

  G   D   G   A
'Til He returns or calls me home

D/F♯   G   Em7 Asus   D
Here in the pow'r of Christ   I'll stand

D/F♯   G   Em7 Asus   D (hold)
Here in the pow'r of Christ   I'll stand

LET EVERYTHING THAT HAS BREATH

MATT REDMAN

Key of **E Major**, 4/4

INTRO:

E5   E5/D♯   C♯m7   Asus2 A/B

E5   E5/D♯   C♯m7   Asus2 A/B   F♯m7 (2 bars)

CHORUS:

E5   E5/D♯
Let everything that, everything that

C♯m7   Asus2   A/B
Everything that has breath praise the Lord

E5   E5/D♯
Let everything that, everything that

C♯m7   Asus2   A/B   F♯m7 (2 bars)
Everything that has breath praise the Lord

VERSE 1:

E5
Praise You in the morning

E5/D♯
Praise You in the evening

C♯m7   Asus2
Praise You when I'm young and when I'm old

E5
Praise You when I'm laughing

E5/D♯
Praise You when I'm grieving

C♯m7   Asus2
Praise You ev'ry season of the soul

PRE-CHORUS 1:

F♯m7   E/G♯
If we could see how much You're worth

F♯m7   E/G♯
Your pow'r, Your might, Your endless love

F♯m7   E/G♯   A A/B
Then surely we would never cease to praise

(REPEAT CHORUS)

VERSE 2:

E5
Praise You in the heavens

E5/D♯
Joining with the angels

C♯m7   Asus2
Praising You forever and a day

E5
Praise You on the earth now

E5/D♯
Joining with creation

C♯m7   Asus2
Calling all the nations to Your praise

PRE-CHORUS 2:

F♯m7   E/G♯
If they could see how much You're worth

F♯m7   E/G♯
Your pow'r, Your might, Your endless love

F♯m7   E/G♯   A A/B
Then surely they would never cease to praise

(REPEAT CHORUS 3X)

END ON E

OPEN THE EYES OF MY HEART

PAUL BALOCHE

Key of **D Major**, 4/4

INTRO (FOUR BARS):

Dsus2

VERSE:

D
Open the eyes of my heart, Lord

A/D
Open the eyes of my heart

       G/D
I want to see You

       D
I want to see You

(REPEAT VERSE)

CHORUS:

       A   **Bm**
To see You high and lifted up

G   **A**
Shining in the light of Your glory

A   **Bm**
Pour out Your power and love

     G   **A**
As we sing holy, holy, holy

(REPEAT VERSE 2X)

(REPEAT CHORUS 2X)

VERSE (2X):

D
Holy, holy holy

A/C♯
Holy, holy, holy

G/B   **G**
Holy, holy, holy

        D
I want to see You

TAG (2X):

D/F♯   **G**   **D**
I want to see You, I want to see You

WORTHY IS THE LAMB

DARLENE ZSCHECH

Key of **G Major**, 4/4

INTRO:

Em7   G   Em7   G

VERSE:

         C   **G/B**
Thank You for the cross, Lord

         C   **D** **G**
Thank You for the price You paid

       D/E   **Em7**   **D**   **C**
Bearing all my sin and shame, in love You came

  Am7 **G/B**   **D**
And gave amazing grace

G   **G/B**   **C**   **G/B**
Thank You for this love, Lord

        C   **D**   **G**
Thank You for the nail-pierced hands

        D/E   **Em7**   **D** **C**
Washed me in Your cleansing flow, now all I know:

    Am7   **G/B**   **D**
Your forgiveness and embrace

CHORUS:

G   **D/F♯** **Am7** **G/B**   **C**
Worthy is the Lamb, seated on the throne

D   **D/C**   **G/B**   **C**   **Am7** **C/G**   **D** **D/F♯**
Crown You now with many crowns, You reign victorious

G   **D/F♯** **Am7** **G/B**   **C**
High and lifted up,   Jesus, Son of God

    D   **D/C** **G/B** **C**   **Dsus**
The Treasure of heaven crucified

      Am7   **G/B** **C**
Worthy is the Lamb

      Am7   **G/B** **Dsus**
Worthy is the Lamb

(REPEAT VERSE)

(REPEAT CHORUS 2X)

TAG:

            Am7 **G/B** **C**
Worthy is the Lamb

            Am7 **G/B** **Dsus**
Worthy is the Lamb

         G (hold)
Worthy is the Lamb